Into the Garden

The Genius of Genesis

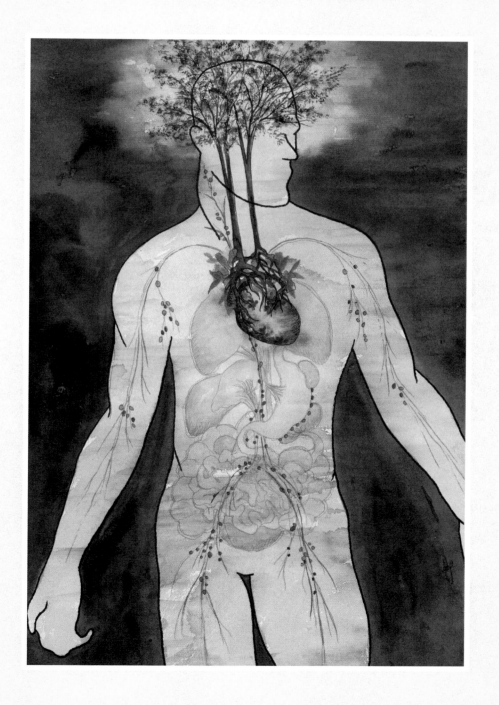

CLAIRE SORDONI

AuthorHouse™
1663 Liberty Drive
Bloomington, IN 47403
www.authorhouse.com
Phone: 1-800-839-8640

All Bible verses have been taken from the King James Version of the Bible.

Published by AuthorHouse 05/11/2015

ISBN: 978-1-4969-3828-2 (sc)
978-1-4969-3829-9 (e)

Library of Congress Control Number: 2014916277

Print information available on the last page.

This book is printed on acid-free paper.

authorHOUSE®

INTRODUCTION

This book offers a symbolic interpretation of the well known Garden of Eden story. The illustrations and comments are the result of a divine dialogue with God in which the content and perspective revealed itself.

The visual investigation presented here illustrates an internal landscape in which we all work with various issues and conditions in our common human experience. It is suggested that Eden represents a physiological map of the human body and that every character in the narrative represents an aspect of ourselves.

The exact translation of Genesis Chapters 1-3 is included from the King James version of the Holy Bible.

GENESIS

CHAPTER 1

In the beginning God created the heaven and the earth.

And the earth was without form, and void; and darkness *was* upon the face of the deep. And the Spirit of God moved upon the face of the waters.

And God said, Let there be light: and there was light.

And God saw the light, that *it was* good: and God divided the light from the darkness.

And God called the light Day, and the darkness he called Night. And the evening and the morning were the first day.

And God said, Let there be a firmament in the midst of the waters, and let it divide the waters from the waters.

And God made the firmament, and divided the waters which *were* under the firmament from the waters which *were* above the firmament: and it was so.

And God called the firmament Heaven. And the evening and the morning were the second day.

And God said, Let the waters under the heaven to be gathered together unto one place, and let the dry *land* appear: and it was so.

And God called the dry *land* Earth; and the gathering together of the waters called the Seas: and God saw that *it was* good.

And God said, Let the earth bring forth grass, the herb yielding seed, *and* the fruit tree yielding fruit after his kind, whose seed *is* in itself, upon the earth: and it was so.

And the earth brought forth grass, *and* herb yielding seed after his kind, and the tree yielding fruit, whose seed *was* in itself, after his kind: and God saw that *it was* good.

And the evening and the morning were the third day.

And God said, Let there be lights in the firmament of the heaven to divide the day from the night; and let them be for signs, and for seasons, and for days, and years:

And let them be for lights in the firmament of the heaven to give light upon the earth: and it was so.

And God made two great lights; the greater light to rule the day, and the lesser light to rule the night: *he made* the stars also.

And God set them in the firmament of the heaven to give light upon the earth,

And to rule over the day and over the night, and to divide the light from the darkness: and God saw *that it was* good.

And the evening and the morning were the fourth day.

And God said, Let the waters bring fourth abundantly the moving creature that hath life, and fowl *that* may fly above the earth in the open firmament of heaven.

And God created great whales, and every living creature that moveth, which the waters brought fourth abundantly, after their kind, and every winged fowl after his kind: and God saw that *it was* good.

And God blessed them, saying, Be fruitful and multiply, and fill the waters in the seas, and let fowl multiply in the earth.

And the evening and the morning were the fifth day.

And God said, Let the earth bring forth the living creature after his kind, cattle and creeping thing, and beast of the earth after his kind: and it was so.

And God made the beast of the earth after his kind, and cattle after their kind, and every thing that creepeth upon the earth after his kind: and God saw that *it was* good.

And God said, Let us make man in our image, after our likeness: and let them have dominion over the fish of the sea, and over the fowl of the air, and over the cattle, and over all the earth, and over every creeping thing that creepeth upon the earth.

So God created man in his *own* image, in the image of God created he him; male and female created he them.

And God blessed them, and God said unto them, Be fruitful and multiply, and replenish the earth, and subdue it: and have dominion over the fish of the sea, and over the fowl of the air, and over every living thing that moveth upon the earth.

And God said, Behold, I have given you every herb bearing seed, which *is* upon the face of all the earth, and every tree, in the which *is* the fruit of a tree yielding seed; to you it shall be for meat.

And to every beast of the earth, and to every fowl of the air, and to everything that creepeth upon the earth, wherein *there is* life, I *have given* every green herb for meat: and it was so.

And God saw every thing that he had made, and, behold, *it was* very good. And the evening and the morning were the sixth day.

INTO THE GARDEN

CHAPTER 2

Thus the heavens and the earth were finished, and all the host of them.

And on the seventh day God ended his work which he had made; and he rested on the seventh day from all his work which he had made.

And God blessed the seventh day, and sanctified it: because that in it he had rested from all his work which God created and made.

These *are* the generations of the heavens and of the earth when they were created, in the day that the Lord God made the earth and the heavens,

And every plant of the field before it was in the earth, and every herb of the field before it grew: for the Lord God had not caused it to rain upon the earth, and *there was* not a man to till the ground.

But there went up a mist from the earth,

and watered the whole face of the ground.

And the Lord God

formed man *of* the dust of the ground,

and breathed into his nostrils the breath of life;

and man became

a living soul.

And the LORD God

planted a garden eastward in Eden;

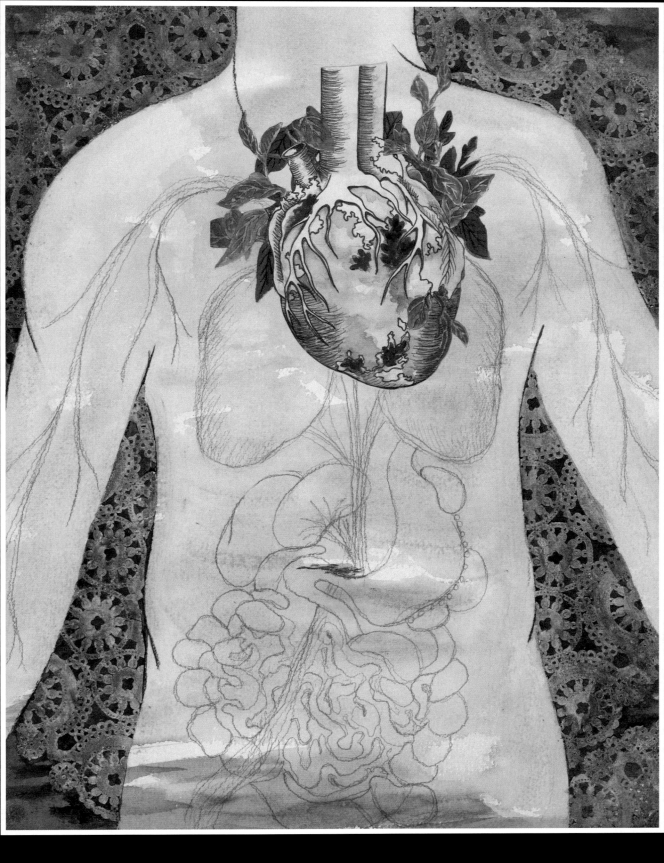

and there he put the man

whom he had formed.

And out of the ground made the LORD God to grow every tree that is pleasant to the sight, and good for food; the tree of life also in the midst of the garden, and the tree of knowledge of good and evil.

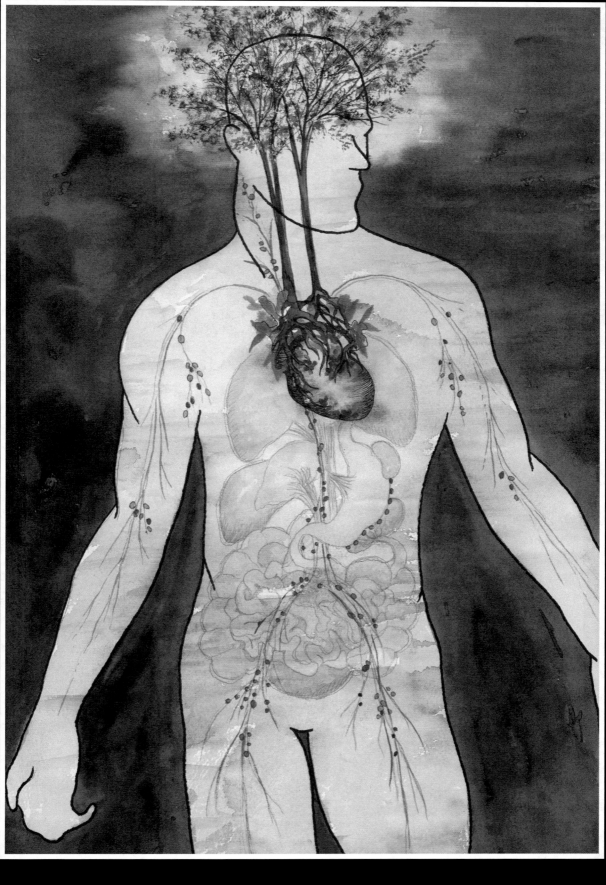

And a river went out of Eden to water the garden; and from thence it was parted, and became into four heads.

The name of the first is Pi'-son: that *is* it which compasseth the whole land of Hav'-i-lah, where *there is* gold;

And the gold of that land *is* good: there *is* bdellium and the onyx stone.

And the name of the second river *is* Gi'-hon: the same *is* it that compasseth the whole land of E-thi-o'-pi-a.

And the name of the third river *is* Hid'-de-kel: that *is* it which goeth toward the east of Assyria. And the fourth river *is* Eu-phra'-tes.

The river that, "went out of Eden to water the garden" is the vital life force, commonly called Prana or Qi. The four rivers extending out of the garden mirror the map of the human circulatory system.

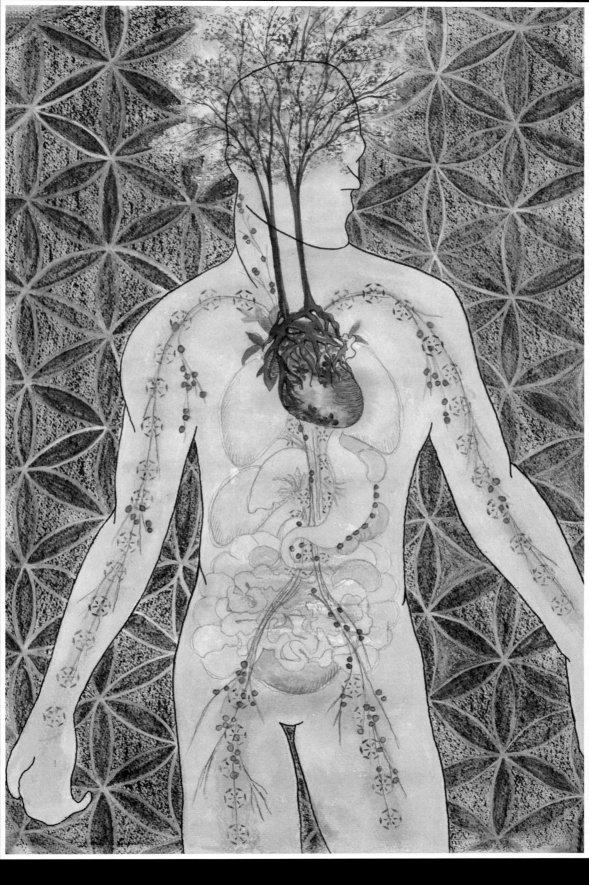

And the LORD God took the man, and put him into the garden of Eden to dress it and to keep it.

This is the second time that God places the man in the Garden. In chapter 2:7 this man is distinguished from the man and woman created in Chapter 1 because he is referred to as a "living soul".

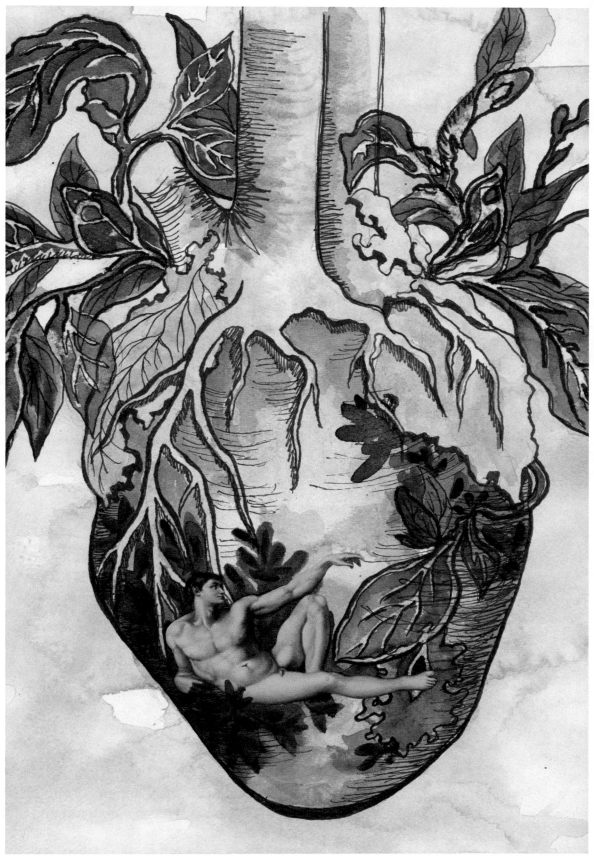

And the LORD God commanded the man, saying,

Of every tree of the garden thou mayest freely eat:

But of the tree of knowledge of good and evil, thou shalt not eat of it: for in the day that thou eatest thereof thou shalt surely die.

The Tree of Knowledge of Good and Evil represents the left hemisphere of the brain. This hemisphere is logical; it separates, files information, judges, and deals with math and reason. It labels and relies on contrast.

And the LORD God said, *It is* not good that the man should be alone; I will make an help meet for him.

And out of the ground the LORD God formed every beast of the field, and every fowl of the air; and brought *them* unto Adam to see what he would call them: and whatsoever Adam called every living creature,

that *was* the name thereof.

Just as God has created man twice and placed him in the Garden twice, in this passage, God creates the animals for a second time.

The animals that Adam names are the emotions he experiences. No single emotion is an equal partner, or "help meet" for him.

This is also the first time man is called Adam.

And Adam gave names to all cattle, and to the fowl
of the air, and to every beast of the field;

but for Adam there was not found

an help meet for him.

And the Lord God caused a deep sleep to fall upon Adam, and he slept: and he took one of his ribs, and closed up the flesh instead thereof;

And the rib, which the Lord God had taken from man, made he a woman, and brought her unto the man.

And Adam said, This is now bone of my bones, and flesh of my flesh: she shall be called Woman, because she was taken out of Man.

Unlike Adam, the woman is created in the Garden.

Therefore shall a man leave his father and his mother, and shall cleave unto his wife: and they shall be one flesh.

The union of the man and the woman describes the union of the masculine and feminine parts within each person.

The masculine part, associated with structure, logic, sequential thought and reason is assigned dependence on the feminine part associated with feeling, adaptability, creativity, impulsiveness and introspectiveness.

It is clear that Adam and the woman are constantly distinguished from each other throughout the entire narrative.

And they were both naked,

the man and his wife, and

were not ashamed.

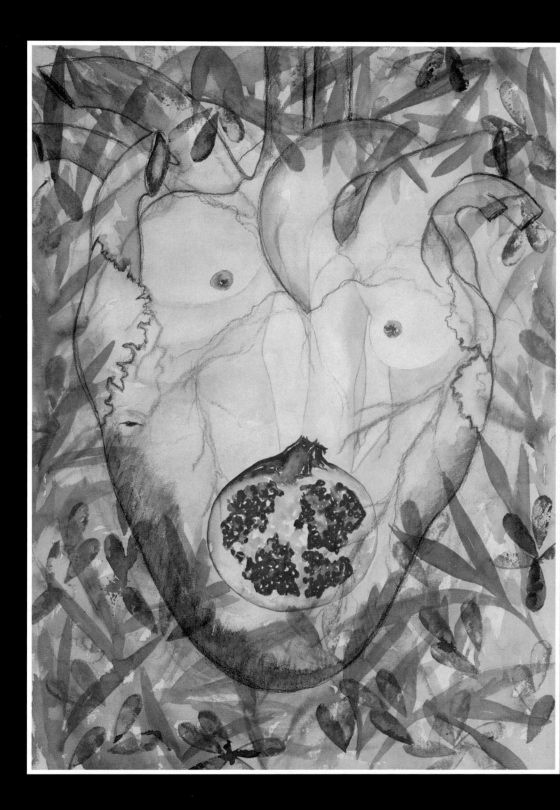

GENESIS

CHAPTER 3

Now the serpent was more subtil than any beast of
the field which the Lord God had made.

The serpent is one of the most misunderstood characters in the entire narrative. In these paintings, the serpent represents the questioning voice within all of us that provokes free will. This constant questioning sometimes exposes a conflict between our desires and intentions. Without this aspect of our psyche, we would not be afforded the opportunity to experience ourselves as identified with our body and its desires, or our soul and its intentions. The serpent is a necessary participant in the relationship between cause and effect. It has always been associated with transformation.

It was not until the New Testament that the serpent was interpreted as the devil or Satan. The concept of original sin also did not exist until several hundred, if not a thousand years later, when the entire narrative was referred to as "The Fall of Man." That interpretation has led to countless generations believing that they are inherently flawed by no fault of their own and has discounted, if not condemned, the contribution of the feminine aspect in all of us.

And he said unto the woman,

Yea, hath God said, Ye shall not eat of every tree

in the garden?

And the woman said unto the serpent, We may eat of the fruit of the trees in the garden:

But the fruit of the tree which *is* in the midst of the garden, God hath said, Ye shall not eat of it, neither shall ye touch it, lest ye die.

And the serpent said unto the woman, Ye shall not surely die:

For God doth know that in the day ye eat thereof, then your eyes shall be opened, and ye shall be as gods,

knowing good and evil.

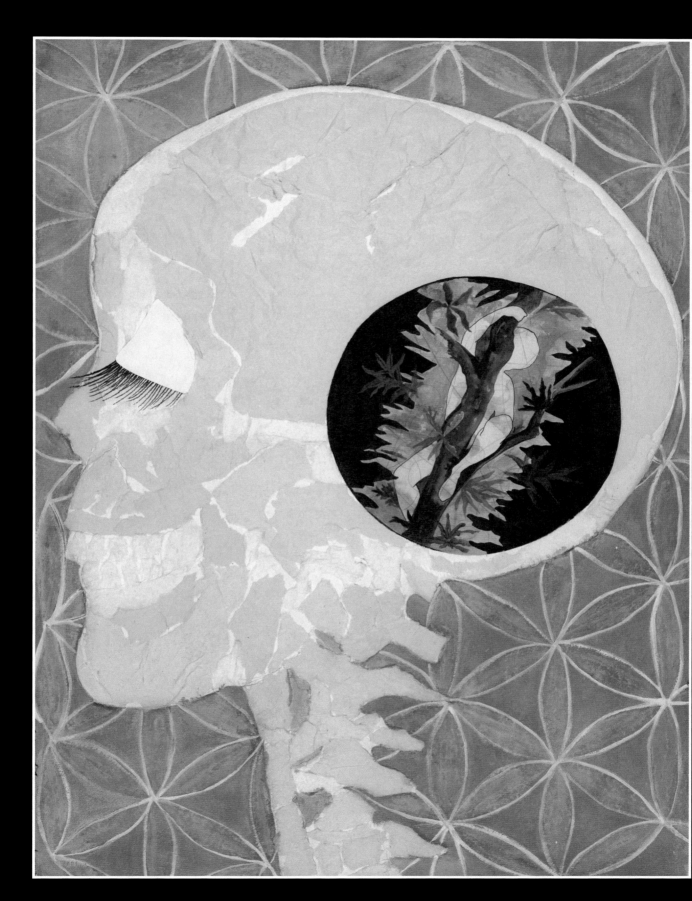

And when the woman saw that the tree *was* good for food, and that it *was* a pleasant to the eyes, and a tree to be desired to make *one* wise, she took the fruit thereof, and did eat, and gave also to her husband with her; and he did eat.

And the eyes of them both were opened, and they knew that they *were* naked; and they sewed fig leaves together, and made themselves aprons.

And they heard the voice of the LORD God walking in the garden in the cool of the day: and Adam and his wife hid themselves from the presence of the LORD God amongst the trees of the garden.

And the Lord God called unto Adam, and said unto him, Where *art* thou?

And he said, I heard thy voice in the garden, and I was afraid, because I *was* naked; and I hid myself.

And he said, Who told thee that thou *wast* naked? Hast thou eaten of the tree, whereof I commanded thee that thou shouldest not eat?

And the man said, The woman whom thou gavest
to be with me, she gave me of the tree, and I did eat.

And the LORD God said unto the woman,

What *is* this *that* thou hast done? And the
woman said,

the serpent beguiled me, and I did eat.

And the LORD God said unto the serpent,

Because thou hast done this, thou *art* cursed above
all cattle, and above every beast of the field;

upon thy belly shalt thou go, and dust shalt thou eat
all the days of thy life:

And I will put enmity between thee and the woman,

and between thy seed and her seed;

it shall bruise thy head, and thou shalt bruise his heel.

There are distinctly different consequences given to the serpent, the woman and Adam.

The serpent is resigned to exist in the subconscious, challenging the creative, feeling, instinctual part of ourselves represented by the woman.

Unto the woman he said,

I will greatly multiply thy sorrow and thy conception;

in sorrow thou shalt bring forth children;

and thy desire *shall be* to thy husband,

and he shall rule over thee.

One definition of conception is, "an abstract idea or mental symbol."

Here, conception refers to the origin of thought and is associated with the word sorrow twice.

There is a distinct reversal in the relationship between the masculine and feminine; the feminine now desires the masculine as opposed to the masculine "cleaving" to the feminine. This reversal represents the submission of the creative, intuitive feminine aspect to the rational, structural masculine.

And unto Adam he said, Because thou hast harkened the voice of thy wife, and hast

eaten of the tree, of which I commanded thee, saying, Thou shalt not eat of it: cursed *is* the ground for thy sake;

in sorrow shalt thou eat *of* it all the days of they life;

Thorns also and thistles shall it bring forth to thee;

and thou shalt eat the herb of the field;

In the sweat of thy face shalt thou eat bread,

till thou return unto the ground; for out of it wast thou taken: for dust thou *art*, and unto dust shalt thou return.

The woman (feminine) was created in the garden, not from the dust of the ground and does not share this consequence. She is never exiled from the garden.

"Cursed is the ground for thy sake" foreshadows the current ecological devastation resulting from the masculine dominating the feminine.

And Adam called his wife's name Eve; because she was the mother of all living.

Unto Adam also and to his wife did the Lord God make coats of skins, and clothed them.

The coats of skins represent the deceptive veils or masks used to conceal vulnerable emotions and ideas.

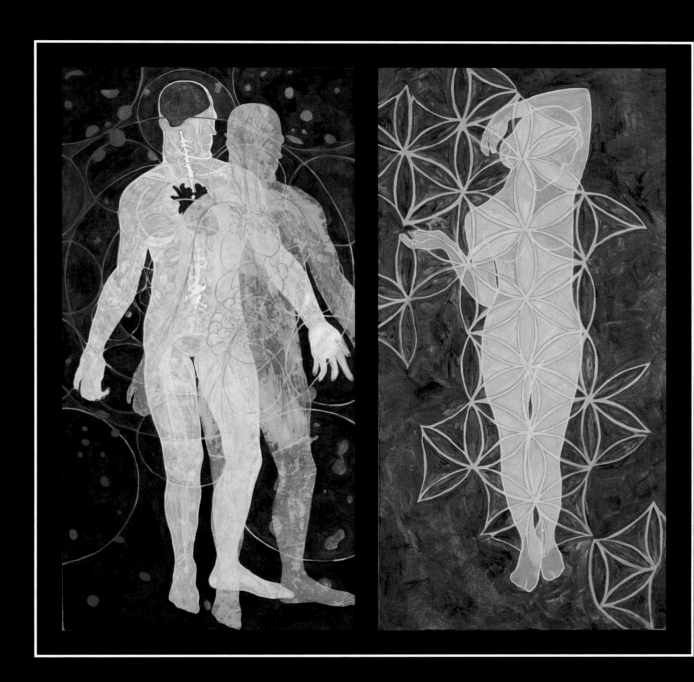

And the LORD God said, Behold, the man is become as one of us, to know good and evil: and now, lest he put forth his hand, and take also of the tree of life, and eat, and live forever:

The tree of life represents the right hemisphere of the brain. This hemisphere is grounded in unity, special perception and creativity. It participates in a harmonious relationship with the heart and Spirit.

Therefore the Lord God sent him forth from the garden of Eden, to till the ground from whence he was taken.

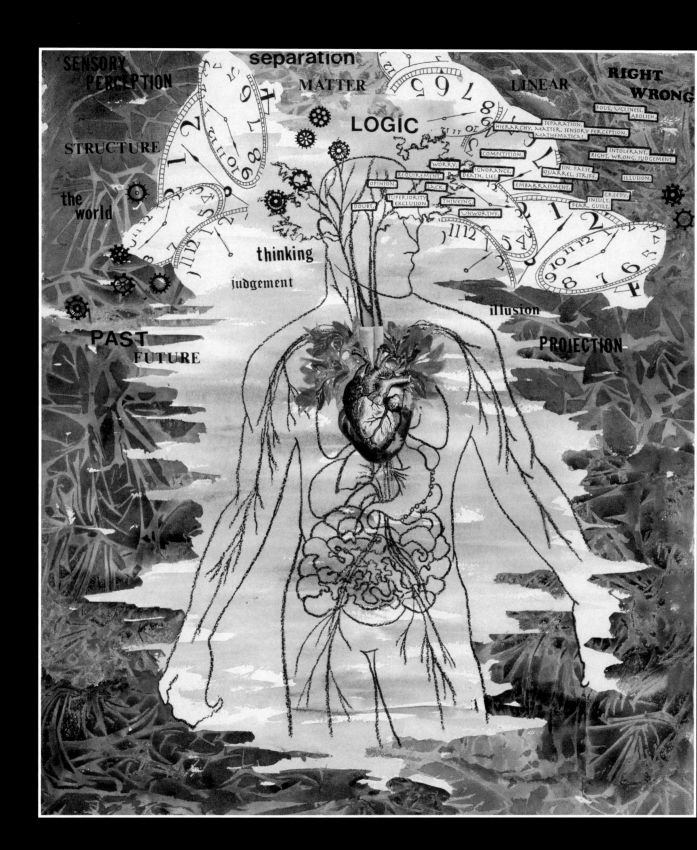

So he drove out the man;

and he placed at the east of the garden of Eden Cher'-u-bims, and a flaming sword which turned every way, to keep the way of the tree of life.

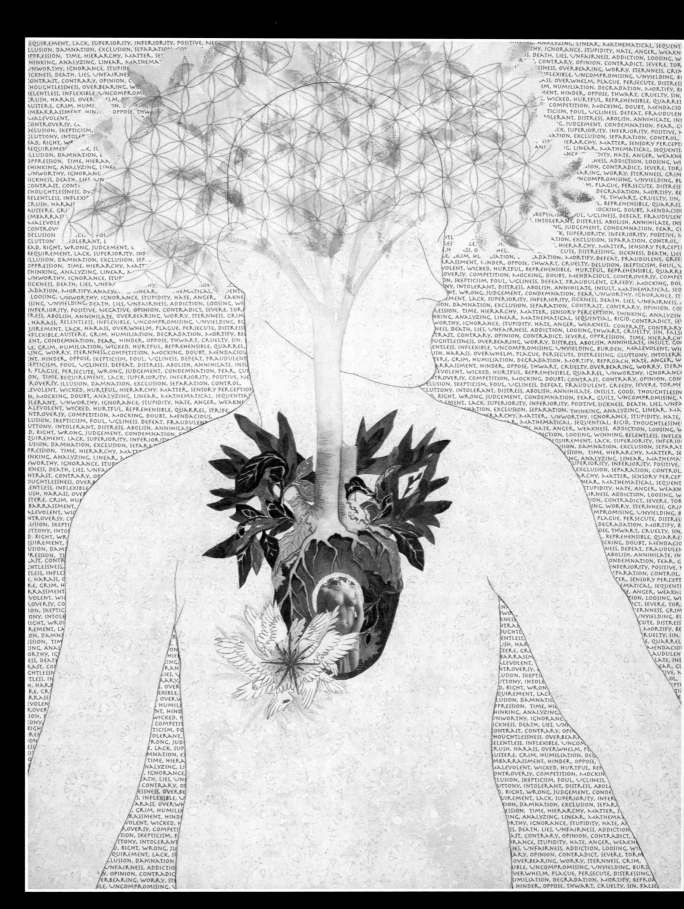

Conclusion

This investigation of the creation story (Genesis, Chapters two and three) challenges every theological, metaphorical and psychological interpretation ever documented.

The work represented here exposes the unsubstantiated and biased views that have influenced western thought; specifically about gender roles and the human experience.

Just as we have made God in our own image, we have imposed our cultural beliefs onto the interpretation of this work.

It has been assumed that Adam and Eve are both exiled from the Garden of Eden, that the serpent either represents satan or sex, that humanity is out of accordance with the will of God, and that the disobedience of women is the explanation for human suffering. All of these ideas are a reflection of cultural memes, NOT a reflection of the words in the biblical text.

Truth is within.

The Garden of Eden story is an explanation as to why we experience ourselves the way we do.

In this illustrated interpretation, Eden is represented as a physiological map of the human body with the human heart as the garden and the rivers mapping the circulatory system.

The internal landscape of the garden includes two trees, representing the hemispheres of the brain and characters representing different aspects of ourselves.

Adam and Eve are the masculine and feminine parts interacting within each person.

The masculine is associated with the physical, structure, logic, matter, judgement and the sensory experience.

The feminine is associated with the creative, adaptive, intuitive, impulsive and feeling part of each person.

The serpent is an agent of transformation and creation, necessary for the experience of free will.

Pain, suffering, ecological abuse and internal conflict are all described as coinciding with the masculine overwhelming the feminine within each person.

Eve was never exiled. The feminine resides in the heart of everyone, while the logical aspect of each person routinely experiences exile from the "garden".

All human beings symbolically experience this narrative within themselves.

It is with great hope that this analysis not only shares the wisdom of Genesis, but redefines the significant contribution of the feminine.

Claire Sordoni is a painter, art teacher, and mother who currently resides in Asheville, North Carolina. She has dedicated her life to nurturing creativity in children and found herself visually interpreting one of the most recognizable and influential stories in the world. Through her own creative process she hopes to inspire her students to pursue their own investigations into art, spirituality, and the nature of the creative process.

Image Credits

While all of the paintings are my original work, I owe credit to various photographers whose influences were invaluable.

I have made every effort to contact the copyright owners and apologize in advance if I have unintentionally left any out. Should it come to anyone's attention that any credit was not properly cited, please contact sordoniclaire@gmail.com so that it may be corrected immediately.

Adam front cover and page 25

Citation:

Michelangelo, "The Creation of Adam" from the ceiling of the Sistine Chapel, Vatican City, Italy

Male outline used on pages 19, 23, 59, 63, 67

Citation:

New Earth Daily. "Our Heart Has a Mind of its Own." http://newearthdaily.com/our-heart-has-a-mind-of-its-own/.

Description: Black-and-white outline of the anatomy of a male with a yellow brain and heart

Statement of use: This image was referenced under the fair use exemption for the purpose of creating new works of art.

Embracing Couple page 35

Citation:

Dreamstime. http://www.dreamstime.com/royalty-free-stock-images-intimate-couple-embracing-image12916579.

Description: Photograph of a man and woman embracing

Statement of use: This photograph was referenced under the fair use exemption for the purpose of creating a new work of art.

Torso of Adam and Eve: page 47

Citation:

Jupiterimages.

Description: Photograph of the naked torsos of a man and a woman

Statement of use: This photograph was referenced under the fair use exemption for the purpose of creating a new work of art.

Eve Reaching: page 55

Citation:

Shutterstock. http://www.shutterstock.com/pic.mhtml?id=26321602.

Description: Color photograph of a naked woman posing with outstretched hand.

Statement of use: This photograph was referenced under the fair use exemption for the purpose of creating a new work of art.

I have been unable to locate the origin of the photographs referenced on pages 47, 49, 51, 53 and the back cover. It is my intention to give credit to these photographers.

If anyone has any information as to the photographs that inspired these paintings, please contact Claire Sordoni at sordoniclaire@gmail.com

Printed in the United States
By Bookmasters